Poetry from the Heart

LEONA MELLO

authorHOUSE®

AuthorHouse™
1663 Liberty Drive
Bloomington, IN 47403
www.authorhouse.com
Phone: 1-800-839-8640

First published by AuthorHouse 9/20/2010

ISBN: 978-1-4520-7436-8 (e)
ISBN: 978-1-4520-7438-2 (sc)
ISBN: 978-1-4520-7437-5 (hc)

Library of Congress Control Number: 2010913851

Printed in the United States of America

This book is printed on acid-free paper.

About the book

Throughout life, we store information collected from
experiences,and try to make some sense of it. Poetry is a very
powerful tool, by which people use to express their feelings.
Whether it be about happiness, loneliness, or just plain life,Poets
write about it. In this book the author simply wants to share her
poetry of something or someone that touched her life in some way

About the Author

Leona Mello born in Bakersfield California where she still resides. She is a full time Mother to three girls and during school she applies her services in helping out in the classrooms. Her poetry is about something or someone who touched her life in some way. Events that took place through out her life and writing poetry is her way to express her feelings on theses events. She has been writing for over twenty years and wanted to share her writings in a book for all to read.

To my Husband Ron and my daughters Allison, Kacie, and Kira. Your love and inspiration helped me to make this book. With all my love I share it with you.

Table of Contents

Loving You

Loving you is really neat
Cause I have someone who's
Really sweet.
Loving you is really grand
Cause I have you to understand
Loving you is something new
Because it's like a dream
Come true
Loving you is just so fine
To have someone who's
Really kind.
Loving you is really straight
Cause you are really
Great
Loving you with all my heart
There is nothing to keep
Us apart
I love you here
I love you near
I love you dear
Forever and ever within
The years

A Weight

A rock I'm not
But a weight I am
With eyes, nose and a smile
Your papers I'll keep in a pile
So look at my face
When you have a mess
And think of a weight
And put me on your desk

Leona Mello

It's All New

To love you
To hold you
It's all new
To talk with you
To teach you
To show you
It's all new
To show you
To grow with you
It's all new
Why is it all new
Because my Darling
So are you.

Tears with Laughter

Tears go
Laughter comes
Tears with laughter is
In everyone
Laughter goes
Tears come
Laughter with tears will
Soon become one

Leona Mello

Nanny

An angel came to take you away
Where skies are always blue
The angel said he'll watch over you
For this we could no longer do
The illness you had took the upper hand
And made us all so blue
We know you're safe
And in place
Where we will soon see you
So at the end we understand
What the angel had to do
And now its time to say goodbye
And we will always love you

A Long Distance Mom

A Long Distance Mom
A long distance mom is
Just a phone call away
We know that she'll be
There every hour of the day
We know that she cares
Which makes it fun when
We have a lot to share
So dry away those tears
And be happy with cheers
Because you know we
Love you
And we know you love
Us too

Leona Mello

To My Sweet Allison

You are my love
Sent from above
You make me laugh
You make me cry
But within a gasp
I turn and smile
I love you so much
And I always knew
God sent you from above
To be here with us
And we will always love you.

To Baby Kacie

It's a day of tears
A day for cheers
You made your entrance
In just nine minutes
Though it was painful
And a little touches and goes
Your here to stay
And you let us know
God sent you to us
And with all our love
We will raise you, and cherish
You as long as we need to
It is a long mile
The life we have
Is really worth while
I love you darling
With all my heart
And with this darling
We will never part

Leona Mello

Life is Like a Balloon

A balloon is filled with air

It flies in the air

The balloon will pop and soon fall down

And no one really cares

A child is born to live

And live a child did

Until one day a child will say

My life will have to end

A balloon filled with air

A child born to live

Will soon rejoin

And take their place

Back on earth again

My Man

Growing old
Growing together
Makes a difference
Just like the weather
Its cold, it's warm. It's misty, it's wet
It' life we share
Even our bed
Growing old is not to bad
When our children have you for a dad
Growing old I understand
I have you for my man
I'll grow old with you
For the rest of my life
And your place will be by my side

Leona Mello

Why can't we do the Rest

The sun rises

The sun sets

The moon rises

The moon sets

The star rises

The stars set

Why in the world can't we do the rest

A Face

A happy face
A sad face
A hurt face
A jerk face
A made-up face
A shape up face
Loving face
A sobbing face
But most of all
It's your face

Leona Mello

I wonder

I wonder about life
Where it will take me
I wonder how high
Is it far, past me
I wonder if you or anyone else
Will take a chance
Inspire of yourself
I wonder if someone really cares
Or is there life at the end of my years
I wonder

Be anything you want

Be a bug
Any kind you want
Big or little
Or even a runt
Say you want to be a grasshopper
And you can jump all around
Or if you were a crawdad
Your feet would never leave the ground
Be a big spider
A little one will do
Spin a web around and around
Write I love you
Be a fly
A little sly
Set on the wall
And watch the world go by
Be anything you want
Grow and Grow
It's a lesson you will learn
Now I have to go

Leona Mello

A Life

A life is given to take a stand

It was a woman

It was a man

Together a life they lived and grew

And created a life that was all new

This new life

He grew and grew

And became a man that no one knew

He found a woman

And took her hand

Now life goes on

As we know and understand

A life is given to each to own

A life was given to take a stand

When I am gone

If you laugh when I'm gone
It is good
If you cry when I'm gone
It is good
Always remember
Your life will go on
And so will I in a different time

Leona Mello

Making a Stand

Making a stand on the world today
To share your thoughts
And learn to pray
Show your courage
To grow through out
Make a marriage to last without
Making a stand to grow and be free
Making a stand to look and see
What you created as the world goes by
A life you see in passer byes

I'll Teach You Things

I'll do my best
I'll raise you right
I'll teach you things
As life goes by
I'll keep you safe
I'll stay close by
I'll teach you things
As life goes by
I'll walk with you side by side
I'll hold your hand so you don't cry
I'll teach you things as life goes by
And in my heart
I will always know
The things I teach you
Will help you to grow

Growing old

Growing old is a way of life
It helps us remember
The time that went by
Growing old is not to bad
With what you left behind
And what you now have
It's good to know that a life you left
Will take your place and do their best
Growing old is a way of life
I'll take a stand right by your side
Growing old
Together we can grow
And make our life memorable

Remember Me

Remember me when I was happy
Remember me when I was sad
Remember me when I was jolly
Remember me when I was mad
If all these things you remember me by
Makes you unhappy
And makes you cry
Than all I ask
Is that you do not remember me at all

Leona Mello

Flunking out of School

I set in class
Trying to grasp
The reading and writing
My teacher was reciting
My mind started to wonder
The words started to thunder
The very thought I had
Was making me sad
Setting and thinking
Of things
To do
I realize I was flunking
Out of school

Inner Peace

I tried to conquer
The best of my life
To hold and cherish
The little lives
The ones I love
That's so dear to me
To hold them tight
So I can see
The things I want
The things I need
To have a life
Of inner peace

Leona Mello

People

Our present is a gift to the world
We are one of a kind
We can make our life what we want it to be
Let's take it one day at a time
Count our blessings
Not our troubles
We'll make it through a day
For whatever comes along
We have something to say
Within us we have so many answers
Understand have courage and be strong
Have health hope and happiness
Take time to wish upon a star
And don't forget
For even a day
How very special we are

20th Anniversary

Twenty years ago we said I do
We stood in the church and I married you
I have no regrets
Our life is great
We have our love to keep us brave
My love for you has never changed
My love for you will stay the same
You are my life along with our girls
You are my star that shines in my world
I love you Ron

What I Give

I give you my love
That goes so deep
I give you my heart
That misses no beat
You have them both
You hold them close
For what I gave
Is yours to keep

I Wish

I wish I had a nickel
For every person I've met
I put it all together
And add it to my list
I wish I had a nickel
For everything gone bad
I put it in a shoe box
And wish for good things back
I wish I had a nickel
For all the wishes I've made
I put it in your hands
Just to be with you today

Leona Mello

Don't Cry for Me

Do not cry for me
For I am not here
Dry your eyes
Wipe your tears
I am not here
Look at the person setting next to you
See my friends and family
I'm there in their hearts
Dry your eyes
Wipe your tears
I am not here
See my Sisters, My brothers too
See my nieces and my nephews
I'm there in their hearts
I'm there in their faces
See my husband, my girls
It's me in their world
Dry your eyes wipe your tears
Do not cry I am here
Here with you in your hearts
Dry your eyes
Cry no more tears for I am not here

Emotions

Emotions of sadness
Emotions of bliss
Emotions of happiness
Just go done the list
Emotions that erupt
Emotions that are calm
Emotions with anger
The list gets long
So many emotions
We put ourselves through
Where would we be?
If we had none of these to do

Nana

Although you got sick
And we knew it was tough
For you to fight
It was just too rough
We miss you so much
Even though you are gone
We know in our hearts
Your true love is strong
So we'll say a prayer
And bless you to God
And see an angel
Stop by for a while
Good bye for now
And we won't forget
Our love
Our hearts
Are sealed with your kiss

Life can Change

An addiction you got
A habit its not
Don't be ashamed
Other people are the same
Look at life
How you want it to be
See how to change
It won't be easy
Think of new things
That you can do
Try to accomplish
What you set out to do
If you fail
Try again
Do not worry
In time you will win

Leona Mello

Let me be your angel

Let me be your angel
I'll watch over you
I'll shelter you from evil
And watch over you
I'll keep you warm
And full of love
I'll be by your side
When you're out at night
Let me be your angel
I'm sent to be with you
I'll keep you safe
And keep watch over you
Let me be your angel
It's the least that I can do

Special Kira Baby

Special as special
As special can be
You are so special
To everyone you meet
To Dad
To Mom
To everyone you know
A special little girl
Who we love so

School

My first day of school
Wasn't so bad
I made new friends
Something I didn't have
I played with blocks
And other toys too
I think I will like going to school
My teacher is nice
She teaches me new things
I learned how to write
Not only my name
We made play dough
It was fun to do
We colored pictures
And listened to stories too
Playing out side
Was a little rough
We had a teacher
That made it a little tough
With all the rules
I still Like School

What are Friends

Mom what are friends
My little girl asked
I looked and smiled
And just had to laugh
A friend is a person
Someone you meet
A friend is nice
And not so mean
A friend you share with
You play with
And have each other
To stay busy with
A friend is a person
Just like you
Someone who cares
And stays close to you
Many people can be your friend
Just open your heart
And let them in

Leona Mello

God

The earth is changing
What can we do
Just believe in God
He'll watch over you
Changes are made
To test our strength
And soon we'll know
The right things to do
Just open your heart
And let him in
God is the one
You need at the end

The Last Day

You would never think the last day will come
A quite rest for everyone
It's time It's now It's here at last
No more waiting
It's all in the past
No more pain will she endure
No more med's will come through the door
She laid and rested for the last time
And in no pain the time went by
The last day has come and gone
And in our hearts her love lives on

How Far

How far is Heaven
How far is God
How will we know
If we go to far
How far is Heaven
How far is God
How will we know
If we don't see the star
How far is Heaven
How far is God
How will we know
If we go to far

A Summer Day

A summer day
In the month of May
Birds are chirping
Trees are turning
The children swing
Mom is burning
The sun is hot
Need to find a cool spot
A summer day
In the month of May
It's May why not

The Lost

A friend of mine had died today
The lost was hard
She could not stay
She's home at last where she lies
With love ones happy to be by her side
No more pain will she endure
God by her side to make sure
Although we miss her sunny smile
We will join her in a while

Does anyone know

What happens to the human mind as we grow old
Does anyone know
What happens to the human body as life goes on
Does anyone know
The mind gets lost
In its own little world
The body gets to tired to move forward
What happens to the person
Who takes on the world
The person gets tired and goes to sleep for good
The mind
The body
The person
Are all combined
In a skeleton of flesh and time

A Beautiful Rainbow

The rain will fall
The wind will blow
Snow will come
This we know
The sun will come
And shine so bright
There is a glow
A beautiful rainbow

Through a Mothers Eyes

They do no wrong
As it goes on in a repeated song
My children are angels
I know this as their mom
They may be spoiled
And have everything they need
They do nothing wrong
Or is it just me
Through a mothers eyes
It's hard to see
The heart ache they cause
And she will disagree
Through a Mothers eyes
We are the best
She picks us up
And dose her best
A child is what a child will be
But through a Mothers eyes
We are kind of unique

Scammed

Do you know how it feels to be scammed

Do people like you under stand

We work real hard on things we do

And people out there take advantage of you

Dose this have anyone's attention

If so I'm glad

Because I am a person

Who dose not likes to be scammed

So go Stay away

Go-Go, Go just scram

Always a Friend

Friendship is without love
Is to love without friendship
And you should receive friendship in return
And may your world be bright
And the sun always gives you light

Leona Mello

My First Day

My first day for the rest of my life
Will never end it just began
Things to see
Things to do
By darkness and by light
Until I know my new life
It will take me places
I'll see new faces
I'll learn new things
And be so gracious
My first day
Will never be the same
When my life begins
And when it will end
My first day
I will always remember
My Father My Mother
Who I love so tender

My God Son

You make me laugh
You make me cry
But above all this
I feel good inside
To know you
To hold you
To watch you grow
A great man you will make
One day I know
Remember my darling
I love you so

I love you

Roses are red
Violets are blue
A star in the sky
Reminds me of you
Your eyes are a light
Your smile how it shines
Your life with me
Is so divine
I love you red
I love you blue
But most of all
I love you

A child is Lost

A child is lost
And may never know
How much you care
And love him so
You do your best
He'll do the rest
Lost may be
A mind set free
He'll never know
How to grow
Only when it's time
For you to let go
That lost child
Will soon be home

Leona Mello

A heavy tear

A heavy tear fell from my eye
I wiped and wiped until it was dry
Why did the tear fall so hard
Because of the pain I have in my heart
Why was there such pain in my heart
Because you left and my life fell apart

Life is like a flower

Life is like a flower
That grows with love
With soil and water
And the sun from above
Life is like a flower
That will die one day
And leave a new life
To take it's place

Leona Mello

A Paper

A paper will fold
On each side
A paper will bend
A paper will tare
A paper won't disintegrate
Into the ground
So keep up your recycling
And keep paper up off the ground

New Year New Life

The day has come
The end is near
A life has begun
And so did a new year
To bring us sorrow
And happiness too
To put aside
The things we didn't do
The day will go
The year will end
Life keep growing
A new year will begin

Linda

God has open his arms
For his Child's return
On angels wings
She did soar
Now at peace
She can rest
And watch over her love ones
At her best

On Angels Wings

On angels wings

She did soar

Back home again

With our heavenly father

No more pain

Will she endure

No more drugs

Will come through her door

Happy now that she's at home

To watch all of us

Who lives below

On angels wings

She did soar

Home again

To live once more

My Mom

Roses for my mom
With a candy heart to boot
Something I can not deliver
So this will have to do
God has you now
And you keep us safe
Your watching eye
Is much to our praise
So here is your rose
And candy heart to boot
For all I can do
Is just visit you

R.I.P. MOM "2007"

Life Continues

Our hearts are breaking
We know we have to stay strong
It's hard to do
When something goes wrong
Just the other day
Someone said do not cry
But what do you do
When a love one dies
So many people
Friends, family and you
Pray to God to help you through
It's a rough road to take
A hard decision to make
God is there for every step you make
Life continues
As did before
There just one more thing
To thank god for
So don't you worry
We'll be just fine
Cause you will always be here
In our hearts and our minds

Leona Mello

Love and Blessings

My love I send to you
Far and wide all true
My family who cares so much
What else can I do
My blessings I give away
To give a love one hope
To ask God to keep them
In my heart so close
My love and blessings
Is all I have
To give my family today
Who God keeps for me
So many miles away

Just Me

I am going to be myself

Happy, sad, mad or mean

What ever it may be

It's going to be

Just me

I'm going to be the person I set out to be

The one that makes me be

Just me

It's not hard to do

Just think

I am myself

The person that you see

It's going to be me

Just me

I am me and I will be

Just me

You will see

Leona Mello

By My Side

By my side
Where you will be
Your smile your laughter
It inspires me.
By my side
Where you will be
Your love your hugs
Is all I need
By my side
Where you will be
Ti l the end of life
You will be with me.

The Call

The Doctor called
He said run, run
Hurry, scurry
And please don't
Worry.
Come, come
The day is done
The time is here
The time has come
Your dad is gone.

R.I.P. Dad 2007

Leona Mello

Friends

Friends come and go
This I know
I have many friends
That are friends till the end
My friends I love
With all my heart
As strong as it may be
Our friendship will never end
Friends

Dad

A team of angels came today
They took your hand
And showed you the way
It's time to go
As a whisper voice says
This we know is true
You could not stay
Now you are at rest
No more suffering will you do
Good by for now
We will miss you
Don't forget our love and hugs
Are sealed with your kiss
As you rise above

R.I.P. DAD 2007

Leona Mello

A Mother

A flower is a Flower
That will last a couple of hours
A mother is my Mother
That will last forever

My child

My child is a Gift
My child is a Life
My child is a Kid
My child is all mine

What God Did and did not Make

God made the trees

God made the seas

God made man

God made woman God made flowers

God made meteor showers

But God did not make murders, drugs, and thieves

The Farmer

I set and watch all day
The farmer who bails his hay
He's tired and tattered
When it comes to
The end of the day
The farmer

As I set in the Park

As I set in the park
I see people walking
I see children playing
I hear dogs barking
As I set in the park
I am wondering
Can life as it is
Be so easy
As I set in the park

What life brings

Life brings happiness
Life brings sadness
Life brings loneliness
Life brings madness
Why is life so hard
It's what we make it
It's our life by far

Leona Mello

If I didn't have you

You brighten my day
With a smile on your face
You give me so much love
With your warm embrace
What would I do
If I didn't have you

If you can't see

If you can't see
That I am hurt
If you can't see
That I am broke
If you can't see
How my heart will mend
Then it is time to end
It is time for you to leave

With Me

The sky stretches from city to city
The roads go from sea to sea
The life we have will last for ever
As long as you are with me
The balloons will float on and on
The trees will blow in a breeze
Our life we have will last for ever
As long as you are with me

Happiness Is

Happiness is not having the best of everything
Happiness is making the best of everything that you have
Life isn't about how we survive a storm
But how to dance in the rain
May your happy day begin with a dance in the rain
Happiness is

True Love

True love is neither physical
Nor romantic
True love is an acceptance
Of all that is
Has been
Or will be
And will not be
True love is where life begins
Or where life ends
True love is
True love

Our freedom

Making a difference
Is not so bad
We fight for our freedom
We once had
We lost our lives
And fought some more
We fight for our freedom
To change our world

I will send

I will send you a wish
A wish of kind
To wish your illness away
And to leave your bad days behind
I will send you a wish
A wish of hope
To wish all good days
Will soon help you grow

In a Classroom

In a classroom
Children set
To learn of a history
That was once set
In a classroom
There is math to do
Who will pass a test or two
In a classroom
Children set
To learn of history
That was once set

A child of eight

Being a child of eight
Is all but great
Sharing,fighting,arguing
Oh what a day
Being a child of eight
Is not so bad
You have each other
When things go bad
Being a child of eight
Now lets get this straight
Being a child of eight
Well it's Great

The ball

The ball is bouncing
The basket is near
Oh my oh dear
What do I fear
The ball is bouncing
The basket is there
In it goes
With nothing to fear

Leona Mello

Just watching

At ten I'm learning
At twenty I'm free
At thirty I'm married
At forty I'm pleased
At fifty a grandma
I learn to be
At sixty I'm sailing
The open sea
At seventy
I'm ailing
At eighty I leave
Now I'm just watching
What you will turn out to be

By my Side

By my side
Where you will be
Your smile you laughter
It comforts me
By my side
Where you will be
Your love your hugs
Is all I need
By my side
Where you will be
Ti 'l the end of life
You'll be with here with me

A Nature Land

A nature land is gone
The fire burned on and on
We tried to save her
But the fire took her
A new nature life
Will soon grow on
A new nature land did grow
A new hope did show
The fire tried
But she survived
And now it grows on and on

Waiting for the doctor

Setting here waiting for the doctor
Is all that I can do
Watching other patients
That are sicker than you
I wonder what if I leave
Will the next one be be sicker than me
Setting and waiting for the doctor
Bothers me

Up Down All Around

Up down all around
Through loops and hula hoops
Up down all around
Changing direction
Changing time
Changing what everything
We do in our life
Up down all around
One day our feet
Will touch the ground

How time fly's

Running around trying to do all that needs to be done
Running around with your feet on the ground
Time will last for everyone
Time will go as we all know
Running around I look toward the sky
Running around boy how time fly's

When you need me

I saw you cry a tear
I wiped you eye
When I was near
I heard you speak
Unspeakable words
To give you strength
I am here
I held you close
What ever it may be
I am by your side
When you need me

Better Days

Better days will have to come
To make it easy for everyone
Better days will come real soon
To help our lives to resume
Better day will soon be here
Now just relax the time is near

Leona Mello

I am There

I am there when you are happy
I am there when you are sad
I am there when you are lonely
I am there when you are mad
If for some reason
I am not there
Always remember
I will be back

The Beach

Strolling along the beach
With the sand beneath my feet
No worries in the world
Just me and my girl
With such a sight
The beach we see
The water by the side
Matches the sky
Strolling along the beach
With the sand beneath my feet
No worries in the world
Just me and my girl
Strolling along the beach

Out side

Go outside and play
I told my kids one day
The sun is out
The sky is clear
It's such a nice day
So go outside and play
Ride your bike
Run the dog
Skip some rope
Go for a jog
The sun is out
The sky is clear
It's such a nice day
So go outside and play

Farmer sleeping

The chickens are clucking
The cows are mooing
The farmers day
Has just begun
The eggs he gets
The cow he milk
The tractor is running
He plow his fields
The day is ending
The cows are sleeping
The farmers day
Is now ending
All is quiet
Work all done
The farmer
Sleeping
Has just begun

A lovely child

The day you were born
I thought of this
A lovely child
I have to kiss
Your life so divine
Your heart so kind
A lovely child
I have in time
Your hugs how they tingle
Your kisses so sweet
A lovely child
Is all I can see

Let it be

Let it be the flowers
Let it be the bees
Let it be the sunshine
That comes and shines on me
Let it be the blue sky
Let it be the clouds
Let it be the rainbow
That sets my worries free

I can not see

Bring me some roses
For I can not see
Bring me some candy
For I can not see
Bring me some music
For I can not see
Roses I can smell
Candy I can taste
Music I can hear
If you bring them to me
For I can not see

The net

Surfing the net
Is what I do
It keeps me busy
All day through
I read my mail
I play my games
I watch some others
Do the same
Surfing the net
Is all I do
It keeps me busy
All day through

A New Me

Give me my coffee
When I rise in the morning
For it should be sweet
Give me some sugar
To stop my yawning
For it should be sweet
A bit of cream
Make it good
And I will be
A new me

Good Bye

The day has come
To say good bye
What will I ever do
I know this way
You could not stay
Whats safe is best for you
So here's a kiss
Upon your cheek
For you to remember me
I know one day
There will be a time
Where we can both be free

Leona Mello

Whats Wrong

Whats wrong mom
Why do you cry
Are you sick
Are you worried
Are you hurt inside
Was it me
Was it him
Has it caused you grief
Let us help
we will do our best
To make you happy
Once again

It Happens all the time

They say gold is heavy
They say silver shines
In this land where we live
It happens all the time
They say that rainbows are lucky
After a good rain we have
They say that people are laughing
In this land where we live
It happens all the time

I write

I pick up my pen
And I write
I write about love
That leaves my sight
I write about people
That passes me by
I write about family
That stands by my side
When I am happy, sad or just being me
I pick up my pen
And I write

My Eye's

My eye's may not see past the opening
My eye's may only see what your showing me
What ever it is I'm sure you know
My eye's for you will always show
The love we have
The life we give
My eye's may not see
But my heart stills lives

Leona Mello

Proud

Six went off to fight
Six returned
With medals they did earn
And two purple hearts too
With their family by their side
You must know how proud
We are of you
The lives they saved
The freedom that rang
What more can they do
You must know how proud
We are of you
Three now gone
After long life lived
Three live on
What more can they give
With family by their side
You must know how proud
We are of you

Breinigsville, PA USA
12 November 2010
249145BV00001B/2/P